Special Effects

Deri Robins

QED Publishing

Copyright © QED Publishing 2004

First published in the UK in 2004 by
QED Publishing
A division of Quarto Publishing plc
The Fitzpatrick Building
188–194 York Way, London N7 9QP

A Catalogue record for this book is available
from the British Library.

ISBN 1 84538 047 9

Written by Deri Robins
Designed by Wladek Szechter/Jacqueline
Palmer
Edited by Sian Morgan/Matthew Harvey
Artwork by Melanie Grimshaw
Photographer Michael Wicks
Thanks to Nicola

Creative Director Louise Morley
Editorial Manager Jean Coppendale

Printed and bound in China

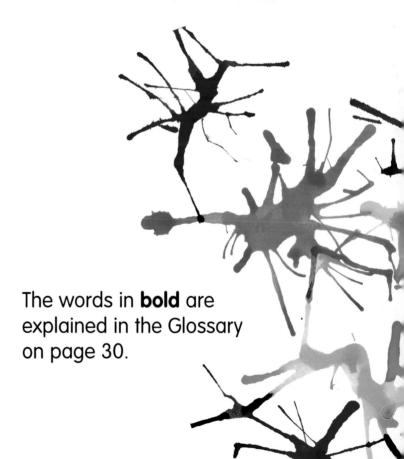

The words in **bold** are
explained in the Glossary
on page 30.

Contents

Tools and materials

This book is all about creating fascinating and unusual art, using a variety of tools and materials. None of the materials is expensive or hard to find: the art kit shown on these pages should enable you to try most of the projects in the book.

Paints

You can make poster paints as thin or thick as you like, so they are ideal for many special effects (see pages 8–15).

Crayons

A number of the art projects use wax crayons. You can use a candle instead of white crayon (see pages 12–17).

Inks

You can get amazing effects using inks, onto both dry and wet paper. Why not try using waterproof inks?

Paper

Try to keep a variety of paper. Thick paper or thin card is better for watery paint, as it is less likely to buckle. **Collages** also need quite thick card. Absorbent paper, such as kitchen towel or blotting paper, greaseproof paper, tissue paper, coloured and **textured** paper are all useful.

crayons

Tools and brushes

Ordinary brushes are useful for details and for paint washes, but you may need some more unusual tools, too. Straws are good for making bubble prints, for blowing paint and for making **quills** from paper. Anything with a sharp point, such as a knitting needle or toothpick, is good for scraperboard pictures or wax transfers. Scissors and glue are essential for collages.

Bits and pieces

Don't throw anything away! You can recycle scrap paper and card, bits of wool and fabric to make collages. Old yoghurt pots and jam jars are useful for mixing paint and cleaning brushes. Newspaper keeps your table clean, and you can cut it up or tear it to use in your pictures!

A camera

There's plenty you can do with photos in art (see pages 28–29). Digital cameras help you to make exciting computer-enhanced art. Throwaway cameras are cheap and light to carry around for spontaneous snapping!

TAKE CARE!

You can do most of the projects in this book on your own. For some, you will need an adult to help. The instructions in the projects will tell you when you need to stop and ask for help.

pencils

sequins

scissors

Hints and tips

A well-organized work station will help you create great art. Find a corner where you can work undisturbed. Give yourself plenty of room to avoid spills and accidents.

Be prepared

Before you start, read through the project and check that you have everything you need. Cover your work surface with newspaper and your clothes with an apron or old shirt – some of the projects can be messy!

Getting ideas

While each of the projects in the book shows you how to achieve a different effect, you will get lots more ideas if you experiment on your own. Test the different effects on scrap paper, and label your results.

Keep an 'ideas scrapbook'. You could stick in your experiments, magazine cuttings, wallpaper, photos, stamps, labels – anything that inspires you!

Collect things!

Become a recycling expert. Always look out for things to use – if you are out walking, bring back grasses, leaves and seed heads; keep old tools, toys, buttons and bits and pieces to use in **collages**, and raid the kitchen for dried pasta or **pulses** (always ask first).

Going further

The special effects in this book make great pictures, but once you know how they work, you can mix and match. For example, cut up a straw painting and use it in a collage or as the **background** for a painting; take a bark rubbing made with crayon and wash it with thin paint to make a wax resist print or you can use collage as part of an ordinary painting.

TIP

A sketchbook will help you record your ideas and **inspiration**. Carry a small sketchbook with you, so that you can make quick sketches for later pictures or jot down notes about your art ideas.

This picture frame has been made using a sea-creature theme.

Using your art work

Many of the special effects in this book can be used to make stunning home-made stationery. Any of the ideas would make wonderful greetings cards. Collage is ideal for covering picture frames cut from card or for decorating mirror surrounds.

Don't throw away spare dripping and dabbing pictures or other decorated paper! Use them to make gift tags or envelopes.

Frame it

Choose your best work to frame and start your own gallery on the wall. Frames can be a simple card border or cut into wild and wacky shapes. You could even continue the pattern of your picture into the frame itself.

If you run out of space on your wall, you can keep your favourite works of art in a folder made of two large pieces of cardboard joined together.

Straw paintings

You can create all kinds of beautiful and mysterious paint effects just by blowing paint – and the results will be different every time.

WHAT YOU NEED
- Straws
- Bright poster paints
- Brushes
- Smooth paper

Did you know, you can make paintings with a straw? Use this effect to create weird and wonderful images.

You can create interesting shapes and images like this tree.

1 Mix up some watery paint. Use a brush to put two large blobs of paint onto the paper. Now use the straw to blow the paint over the paper to make wiggly lines.

2 Let the first colour dry. Repeat the process with different colours until you have an image.

Guess the shape

When you make straw paintings, it is fun to start without knowing what picture you are going to create. Just start moving the paint around and wait for a shape to start appearing.

If you get an idea of what your picture could be, start adding touches to finish it off. For example, a bird would have legs, eyes and a beak. Use this technique as part of a painting to create hair, a mane or the branches on a tree.

TIP

Straw painting is great for making colourful star pictures. Just use lots of small blobs of paint in different colours.

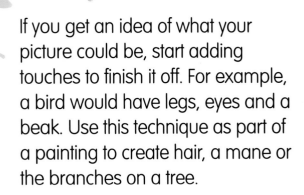

Dripping and dabbing

Add blobs of paint or ink onto wet paper to make stunning patterns and paintings. You can even use felt tips and food dye!

1 Tape the paper to a piece of board to stop it wrinkling. Wet the paper with a large brush dipped in water.

2 To make the petals of an open flower, drip blobs of paint in a circle. Single blobs make good flower buds. Let the paint spread and dry.

3 Use a thin brush to add leaves, stems and **stamens**.

4 Add a soft colour as a **background**. If you put drops of water onto the paint, you will get a dappled effect.

TIP

Experiment with different watery paint effects. What happens when you add a blob of paint to another colour that is still wet? Try some different colours.

Wax resist

Waxy crayons and watery paints don't mix – which means that if you draw a picture in crayon and then paint over the top, the drawing will show through.

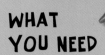

WHAT YOU NEED
- A white wax crayon
- Paper
- Poster paints

1 Use the wax crayon to draw the outline of the marrow and add some lines running along it.

2 Paint yellow paint over the wax. The wax will resist the paint and the drawing will show through.

3 Let the yellow paint dry. It will settle between the wax lines.

4 When the yellow paint is dry, add some more wax lines.

5 Add green paint. The wax allows the yellow to show through.

Scraperboard

While watery paints slide off wax crayon, you can get quite different results if you cover the whole area with thick paint, and then scrape patterns in the surface.

Make your own scraperboard

1 Cover the paper with crayon, without any gaps. Whatever colour you use will show through – so choose bright colours, or a white candle.

2 Now brush thick, black paint over the crayon surface, and leave it to dry. Repeat two or three times until the crayon is completely covered.

Making pictures

3 Scrape a pattern in the surface of the board, using various tools – try the end of a paintbrush, a lollipop stick or a knitting needle.

TIP

Experiment with different scraperboard techniques. Instead of covering the crayon with black paint, use dark crayons and then cover them with white paint – black showing through white is very dramatic.

TIP

You could also try making lots of small scraperboard pictures rather than one large one. Try using lots of different colours of crayon – diagonal lines of red and orange make great flickering flame effects.

Wax transfer

You can use wax crayons to make home-made transfers. Try out some simple designs, such as flower shapes, then when you have practised this technique you can go on to make more detailed, colourful pictures.

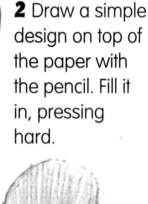

1 Cover part of a piece of paper with thick crayon. Lay a clean piece of paper on top.

2 Draw a simple design on top of the paper with the pencil. Fill it in, pressing hard.

3 Lift off the paper. The crayon should have transferred to the underside of the top piece of paper, leaving a pale copy on the piece below.

Colour transfer

Using this wax transfer effect, you can turn a simple **silhouette** into an unusual colourful picture.

1 Lightly draw or trace a design on one side of the greaseproof paper. You don't need to keep the shapes simple.

2 Turn the greaseproof paper over, and colour it with different-coloured crayons. Try bands of colour, splodges, circles or squares.

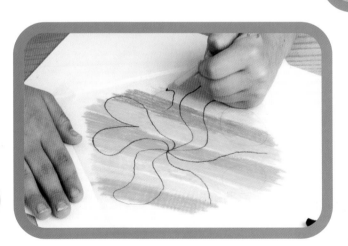

3 Place the paper, crayon-side down, on a clean sheet of paper. Tape the edges so it doesn't slip. Now go over all the lines and areas of solid colour with the pencil, pressing firmly.

4 Lift off the greaseproof paper to see the wax transfer beneath.

Glitter glue

Glitter comes in lots of different colours and can be used to make wonderful, sparkling pictures. Try this rocket idea.

Paint and sparkle

In this project, you use glue like paint to draw the shapes you want in your picture. Before the glue is dry, add some sparkle!

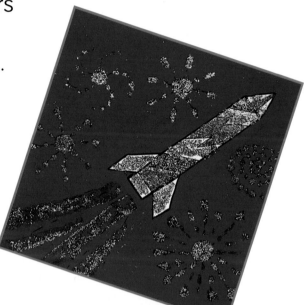

Try making this rocket picture first. Then think of some other pictures that would look good in glitter.

WHAT YOU NEED
- Coloured paper
- Pencil
- Glitter
- Glue
- Brush

1 Draw the outline of the shapes in your picture in pencil. These are just guides for the glue stage.

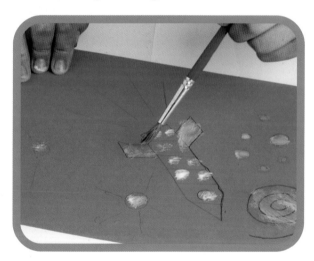

2 Use the brush to paint glue into shapes. You could just use blobs or fill the shapes in fully.

3 Before the glue dries, pick up some glitter and sprinkle it onto the picture. Use different coloured glitters for different areas so that the finished picture is bright. Leave the glitter on for a few minutes, before blowing off the extra glitter. The rest will have stuck to the glue and made a colourful image.

TIP

You could make your own glitter paint. Just mix some glitter with some glue and use a brush to put the sparkly paint on your paper. Now you can make your own glittering masterpieces.

Fabric collage

So far, the art projects in this book have used paints, crayons and inks. But you can also make fantastic pictures using fabric.

A material world

Using fabric to make a picture helps to make lots of interesting textures and shapes. Try this country scene.

1 First, sketch the outlines of the scene on your paper in soft pencil. It is best to use card or thick paper as normal paper might tear.

2 Cut out the large background pieces of fabric. You'll need blue for the sky, dark green for hills and light green for the fields.

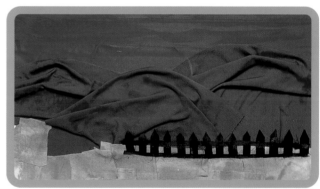

3 Now start adding details: a fence, a hedge, trees, animals in the fields, clouds and some flowers.

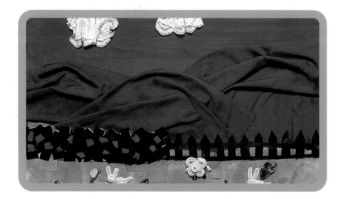

TIP

Collect old bits of fabric for your pictures. Scraps of white lace are excellent for making clouds or snowy scenes. Ribbons are handy for creating flowers. Experiment with different fabrics for making different objects.

TIP

When you have finished your fabric **collage**, you can paint it with clear varnish. This adds great depth and makes the surface of the picture shine. The varnish effect looks great on a dark background.

Paper sewing

Sewing isn't just for fabric. You can also use your needle and thread to make great designs on thick paper or thin card. Always ask an adult for help when you want to use a needle. You could even use sewing in one of your paintings!

Embroidery house

This simple project will show you the basic method of paper sewing. Try some other designs.

1 Draw a simple design on paper. Tape this over the piece of card, and sew thread through the paper and into the card. Throw the paper away.

2 On the back of the card, tidy up the loose threads. Knot the ends, cut the **excess** and put small pieces of sticky tape over the joins.

3 Finally, cut another piece of card slightly larger than the one with the sewing on it. Glue the sewing picture onto this.

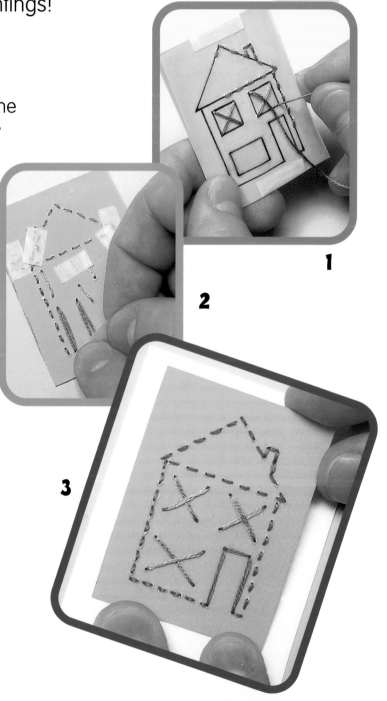

1

2

3

Stitching decorations

There a lots of variations you can use with paper sewing. Try putting colourful beads onto the thread and making zig-zag patterns. You can use thread to make decorative borders to your cards and letters – just make sure you use thick enough paper to hold the thread.

Paper pricking

You could also just use the needle to make holes in the paper that show up when light shines through them. This is a technique called paper pricking.

TIP

See if you can use sewing in some of your paintings or **collages**. You could use thread to make hair, colourful plants in the garden or even a waterfall. Use different colours of thread together to get interesting results.

As well as decorative borders, you can use sewing to make colourful designs for birthday and Christmas cards. Using the same method as the project on page 22, you can make any shape or design you like.

Collage

Paper and card is cheap, colourful and easy to cut and paste, which makes it perfect for **collage**. Keep as many scraps as you can find – you never know when they may come in useful!

WHAT YOU NEED
- Colour paper, magazines
- Paper or card
- Glue

Making a collage

1 Sketch out a design on a piece of card or thick paper.

2 Cut or tear paper shapes to make up the design.

3 Arrange the pieces of paper until you are happy with the way they look and glue them in place.

Mosaic

Try some different techniques in your collages. What about cutting out lots of small, coloured squares from old magazines and making them into an image like a Roman **mosaic**?

Experiment with other materials, too, such as buttons, silver foil and newspaper. You could also paint bits of paper different colours, tear them up and then use them in your collages. Torn paper creates interesting textures.

Here is another colourful collage made with different types of paper.

You can tear paper into the shape of animals, flowers and trees.

TIP

Once you have used paper to make colourful collages, you can go on to make paper **sculptures**. Cut out the shapes you'll need for your design, then colour them before you glue them together. You can make hair by cutting thin strips of paper.

You could even make a sculpture out of paper.

25

Bits and pieces

Bits and pieces from around the home look great in **collages**: scraps of fabric, lace, **sequins**, pasta, **pulses** and even tools. You could probably make a collage from the contents of your wastepaper bin!

WHAT YOU NEED

- Fluffy feather
- String
- Cocktail sticks
- Coloured paper
- Dry leaves
- Bead
- Rice
- Cardboard

Perfect pets

1 Draw the outlines of your picture with a pen then cut them out. Cut just inside the lines, so that the pen marks don't show – or turn them the other way round.

2 Arrange the main shapes on the cardboard. When you are happy with the way they look, glue them down.

3 Now add a bead for the eye, rice flowers, cocktail sticks and string for the fence, coloured paper for the apples and feathers for the mane and tail.

Still life

All the ingredients in this collage are easy to find. You could adapt it by mixing the collage with painting, and adding other natural things, such as dried beans, seeds and pulses.

1 Think how you could make what you've collected into a collage. Sketch the design on a piece of thick paper or card.

2 Arrange your collection on the pencil outline. Glue it in place.

3 You could leave your collage as it is. Or paint in a **background** and some flowers among your collage flower heads. Try adding colour to some of the objects in the collage if you like.

Using photos

A camera can be useful in art. You can get all kinds of unusual effects if you combine photos with painting and **collage**. Keep your eyes open for interesting shots, and save photographs from magazines.

Fantasy fun

1 Fancy a change of scene? Take a photo of your house and paint an unusual **background** to make it look as though you live somewhere different. Look in travel brochures for some **inspiration**.

2 Cut out the house and glue it to the background, or **superimpose** it using computer software. Send it as a postcard to family or friends.

3 What about adding a friend or a pet to your picture? You could have fun playing with size and **proportions**, too! In your fantasy picture, objects can be as big or small as you like.

Picture strips

1 Find two photos or magazine pictures, roughly the same size, and divide them into equal sections of 2.5cm.

2 Cut along the lines to make neat strips.

3 Now glue the first strip from the first picture onto some card, followed by the first strip from the second picture. Keep going until you've used all the strips.

You can use this effect to mix different animals, or alternate an animal with a photo of a celebrity or a landscape.

Try cutting the strips diagonally and horizontally, too.

Glossary

background   the area of a picture behind the main object – for example, a field and distant hills

collage   making pictures or patterns using different materials such as paper, cloth and photographs, which are glued onto a background

embroidery   making pictures or patterns with sewing

excess   the extra bits that you do not need

inspiration   when you get an idea for a picture

mosaic   a picture made up of lots of small squares of colour

proportion   when things are made to look the right size in a picture

pulses   seeds that can be cooked and eaten

quills   curled-up pieces of paper

sculptures   art made by carving or constructing objects

sequins   small, shiny pieces of metal or plastic, often used in sparkly dresses

silhouette   when an object is seen against a light background, with just the outline visible

stamen   the long, thin part in the centre of a flower

superimpose   to put one thing on top of another

texture   the way something feels – for example, it could be rough or smooth

Index

Notes for teachers

The projects in this book are aimed at Key Stage 2 children. You can use them as stand-alone lessons or as a part of other topics or subjects.

The ideas offer children inspiration, but you should always encourage them to draw from their own imagination and first-hand observation as well as from memory and their own experience.

Sourcing ideas

All art projects should tap into children's interests, and be relevant to their lives and experiences. Some stimulating starting points might be: found objects, discussions about their family and pets, hobbies, TV programmes or topical events.

Encourage children to source their own ideas and references, from books, magazines, the Internet or CD-ROMs.

Digital cameras can create reference material (pictures of landscapes, people or animals) and also be used alongside children's finished work (see below).

Other lessons can often be an ideal springboard for an art project – for example, an investigation into your local area could result in a class collage, a field trip could yield rubbings for a wax and resist project and mosaics fit into history projects.

Encourage children to keep a sketchbook of their ideas, and to collect other images and objects to help them develop their art.

Give pupils as many first-hand experiences as possible through visits and contact with creative people.

Evaluating work

It's important and motivating for children to share their work with others, and to compare ideas and methods. Encourage them to talk about their work. What do they like best about it? How would they do it differently next time?

Show the children examples of other artists' work – how did they tackle the same subject and problems? Do the children like the work? Why? Why not?

Help children to judge the originality and value of their work, to appreciate the different qualities in others' work and to value ways of working that are different from their own. Display all the children's work.

Going further

Look at ways to develop projects – for example, many of the ideas in this book could be adapted into painting and print-making. Remember to use image-enhancing computer software and digital scanners to enhance, build up and juxtapose images.

Show the children how to set up a class art gallery on the school website. Having their work displayed professionally makes them feel that their work is really valued.